ANTHEM EASTER I

with

QUESTIONS: A LULLABY CAROL

MUSIC BY DAVID GOODE

WORDS BY FRANCIS WARNER

2019

Published 2019 by Colin Smythe Limited
38 Mill Lane, Gerrards Cross, Buckinghamshire, SL9 8BA
www.colinsmythe.co.uk

Picture Credits:
Convento di San Marco, Florence:
Fra Angelico: fresco, Noli Me Tangere (*details*) pp.1, 5, 25; (*in full*) p.39

Galleria degli Uffizi, Florence:
Gentile da Fabriano: Rest during the Flight into Egypt (*detail*) p.6
Lorenzo di Credi: Adoration of the Shepherds (*detail*) p.7

The photograph on page 43 reproduced by kind permission of
The Rev'd Canon Emeritus Andrew C. Warner

Manfred Grohe © NouvellesIMAGES S.A. et Voller Ernst 1995:
La famille cygne (*endpiece*)

Cover photograph © Billett Potter, reproduced by kind permission of the
Provost and Fellows of King's College, Cambridge

Anthem recording © 2019 by kind permission of the
Provost and Fellows of King's College, Cambridge

Carol recording © 2017 by kind permission of the
Provost and Fellows of Eton College

British Library Cataloguing-in-Publication Data
A catalogue record for this book is available from the British Library

ISBN 978-0-86140-503-9

Text prepared by Anne Millard
Co-ordinator: Margaret Hebdon
Designed by Libanus Press, Marlborough
Printed by Hampton Printing (Bristol) Ltd

CAROL and ANTHEM

David Goode's

QUESTIONS: A Lullaby Carol

was first performed during the Eton College Carol Service 2011
by the Chapel Choir
Director of Music: Tim Johnson
This recording was made by the choir 15 January 2017

The première of

ANTHEM FOR EASTER DAY

was performed by the choir of King's College
in chapel on 12 May 2019 (Organist: Henry Websdale)
Director of Music: Sir Stephen Cleobury

David Goode, Stephen Cleobury and
Francis Warner, King's College Chapel
12 May 2019

For Penelope
who shared it all

QUESTIONS

A Lullaby Carol

QUESTIONS
A Lullaby Carol

The wet nose of the donkey
       The wet warmth of your breast –
But what strange shadow leans over
       My strawy nest?

Young farmhands come to bless my sweet
       With freshness from the field.
Like butterflies that wake too soon
       Your eyelids yield.

The roofbeams bear the winter
       Of all the wilding world;
I see them, and the shepherds –
       But what strange scurry swirled?

Your father scrapes snow from the door
       As politicians shed
Wonders I do not understand
       About our bed.

Mother, the lamb is crying
    We both of us need milk –
Who is that last that brushes us
    With midnight silk?

We cannot understand, my babe,
    These strange foreshadowings.
Now all have left, come take my milk;
    Sleep, while your mother sings:

Lullaby, lily-lullay,
Hold my finger in your palm
Tight now all the world is still.
Stay you safe from cold and harm
As within your father's arm
Sleeps the lamb brought from the hill.

QUESTIONS
A Lullaby Carol

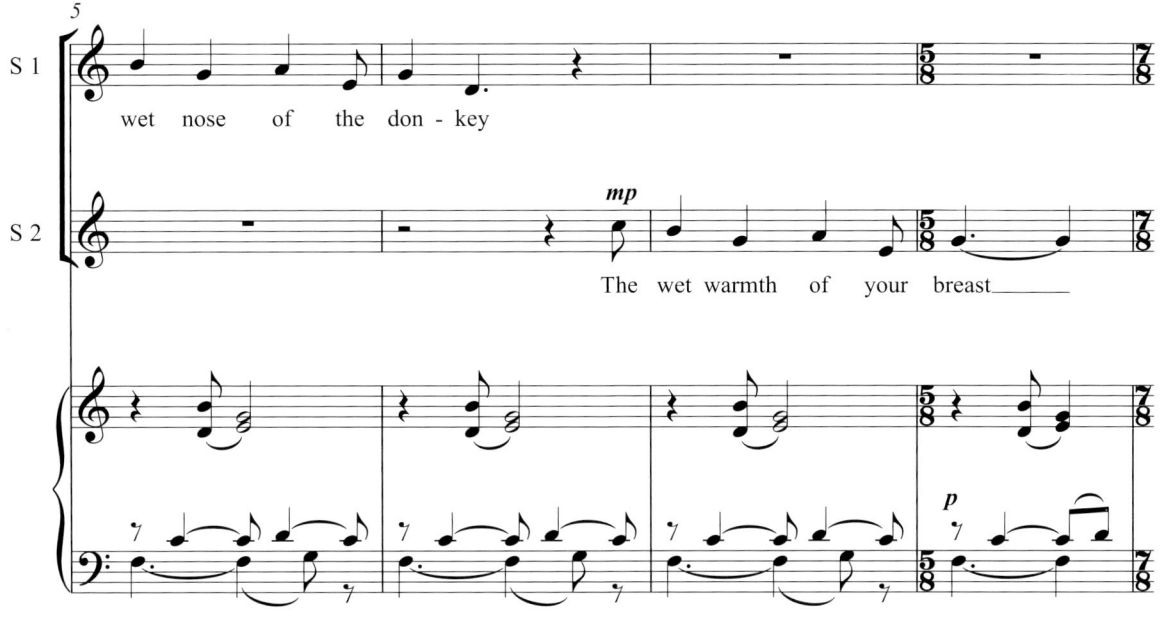

wet nose of the don - key

The wet warmth of your breast

But what strange sha-dow leans ov - er My straw - y

But what strange sha-dow leans ov - er My straw - y

winter of all the wild - ing world_____

I see them, and the shep - herds   But what strange scu - rry

I see them, and the shep - herds   But what strange scu - rry

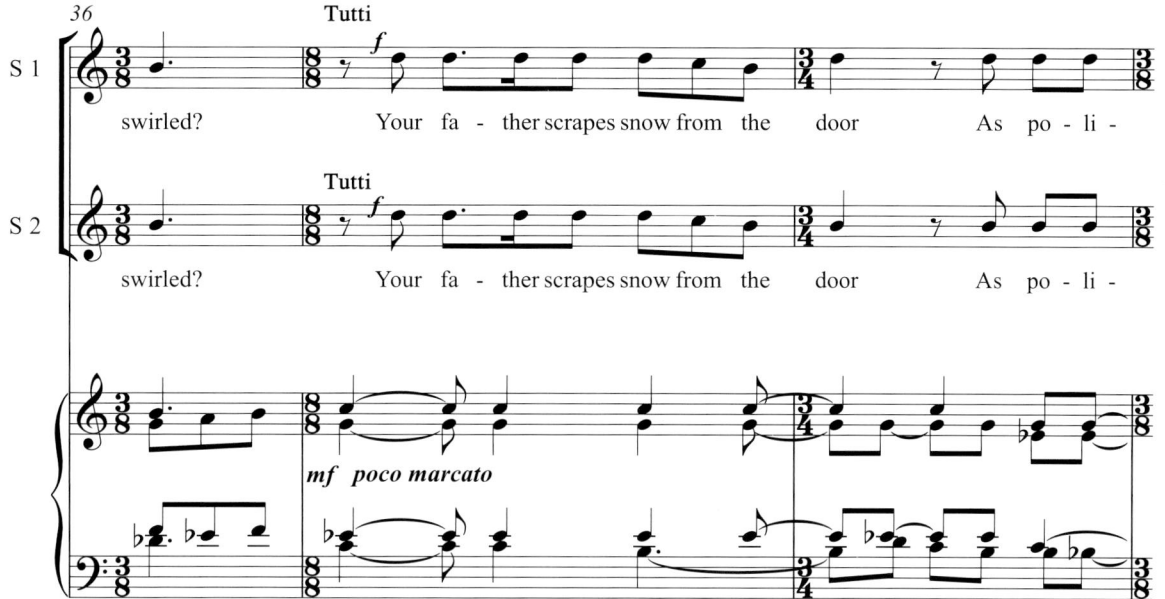

swirled?   Your fa - ther scrapes snow from the   door   As po - li -

swirled?   Your fa - ther scrapes snow from the   door   As po - li -

ti - cians shed   won - ders   I   do   not   un - der - stand

ti - cians shed   won - ders   I   do   not   un - der - stand

a-bout our bed.

a-bout our bed.

-by, lul - lay,

-la - by, -ly lul - lay,

Lul - la - by, Li - ly lul - lay,

Solo

Mo - ther,_____ the lamb is cry - ing_

16

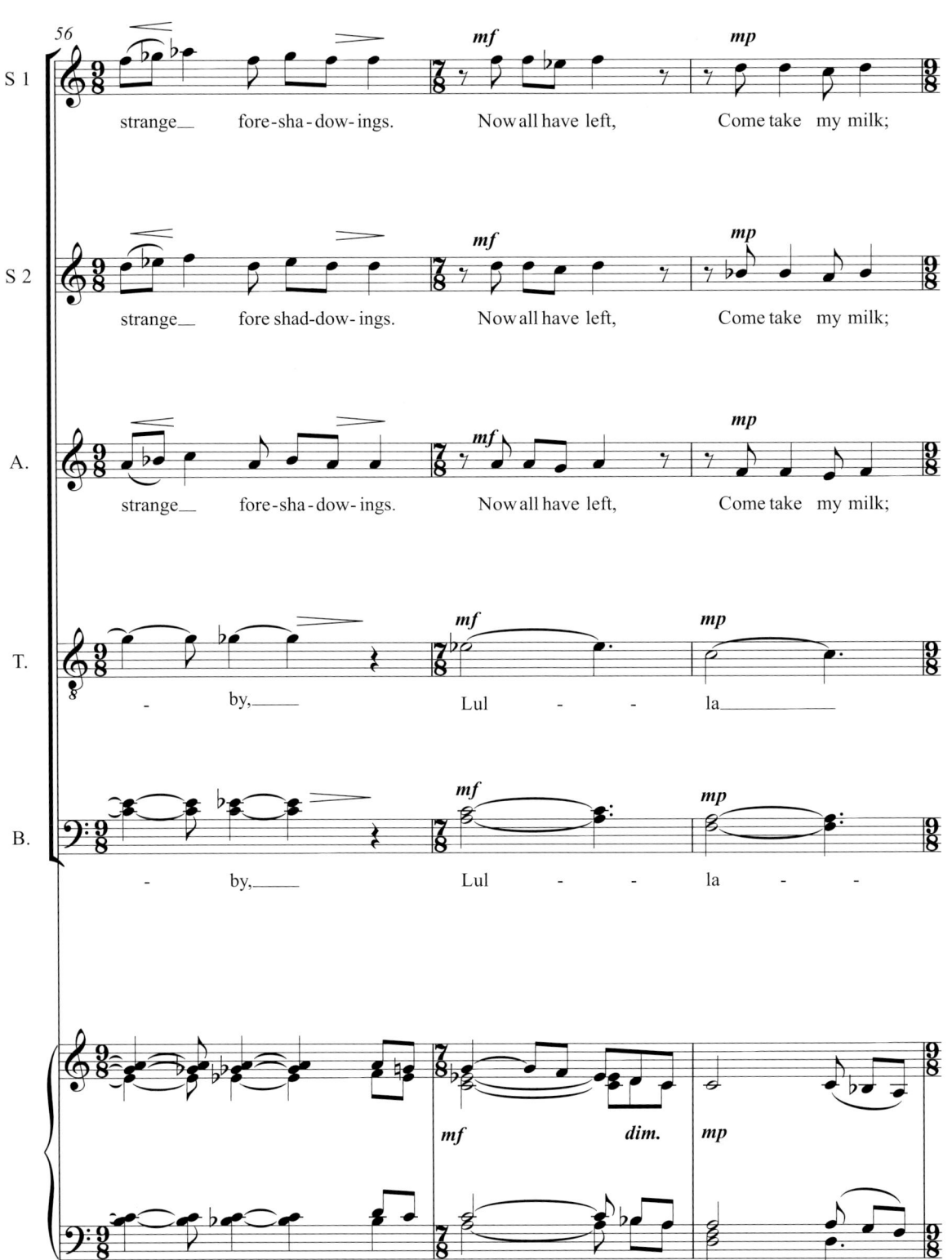

world is still. Stay you safe from cold and harm As

ANTHEM
FOR EASTER DAY

ANTHEM FOR EASTER DAY

Even as a swan enfolds within her wings

Her cygnets on her back, penned in love's care,

So He, pure as a blackbird when it sings,

Like a white flame drew us towards his flare.

The full moon pressed sharp shadows through the trees

As evil strained to force goodness despair.

Lies backed by violence make the blood freeze.

What followed is too terrible to bear.

When darkness bleeds, lanced by the orient

In dawn's first freshness, green stalks lift to play

Through soundless dew soft orchestras of scent

As flowers open to the spring of day

    I was in tears: nothing would be the same.

    Just then the gardener spoke one word: my name.

ANTHEM FOR EASTER DAY

drew us___ to-wards___ his flare.___

drew us to-wards his flare.

us to - wards his flare.___

us to - wards his___ flare.___

30

25
mp, espr.
The full moon pressed sharp sha - dows
p, distinto
poco cresc.
The full moon pressed sharp sha - dows through the
p, distinto
poco cresc.
The full moon pressed sharp sha - dows through the
p, distinto
The full moon pressed shad-ows, sharp shad - ows through the trees,
31
poco a poco stretto
mf cresc.
through the trees As ev-il strained to force good-ness des-
mf cresc.
trees As ev-il strained to force good-ness des-pair.
mf cresc.
trees As ev-il strained to force good-ness des-pair.
mp cresc.
mf cresc.
the trees As ev-il strained to force good-ness
poco a poco stretto
3
mp
f

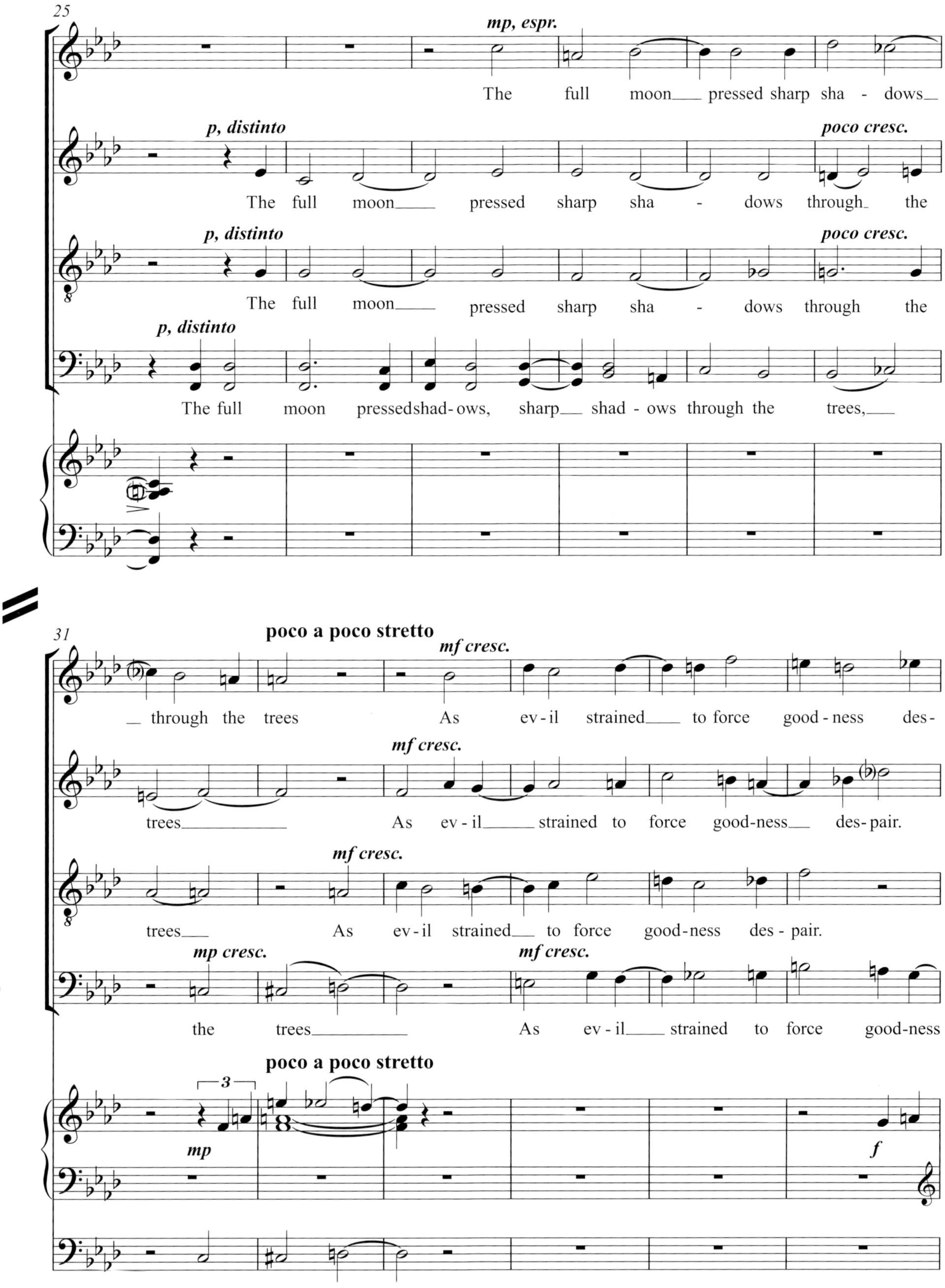

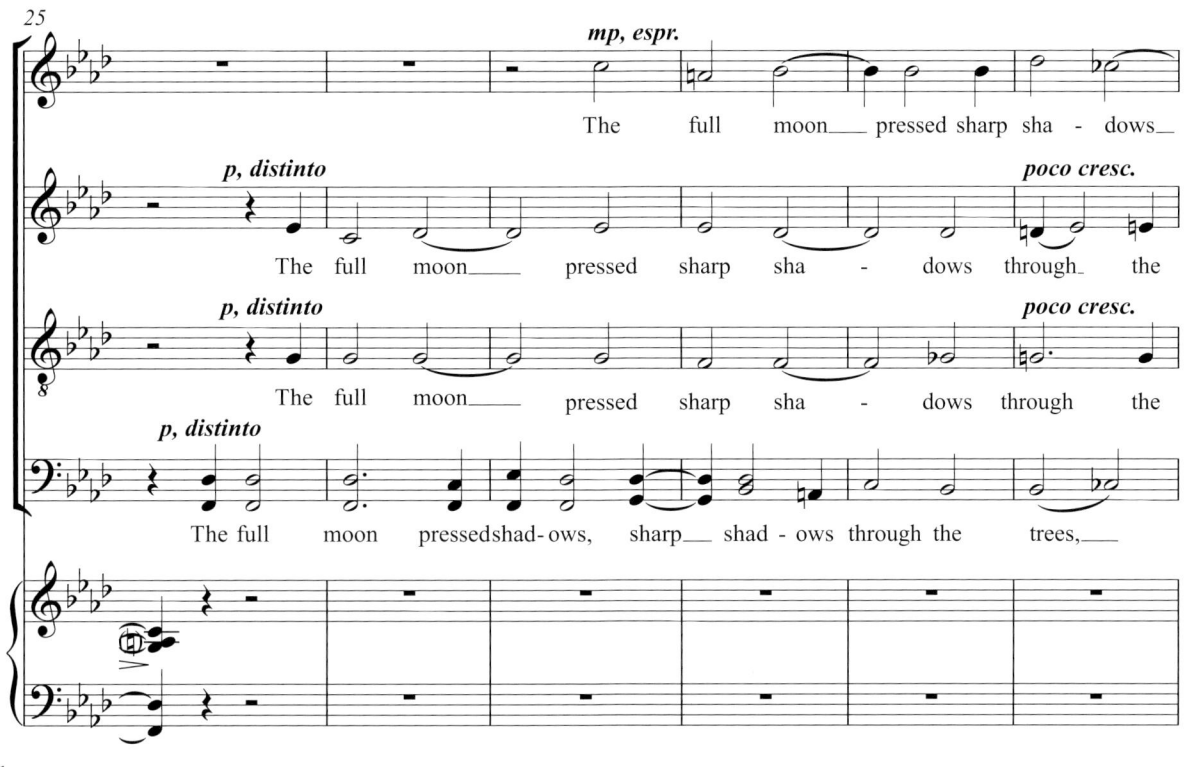

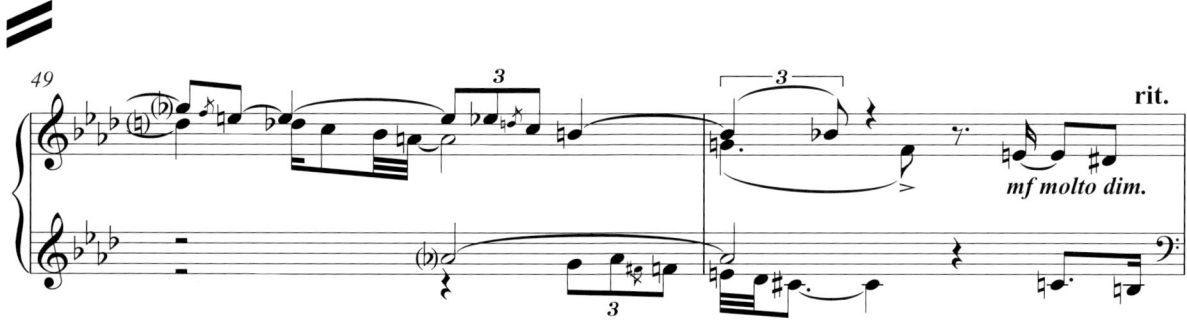

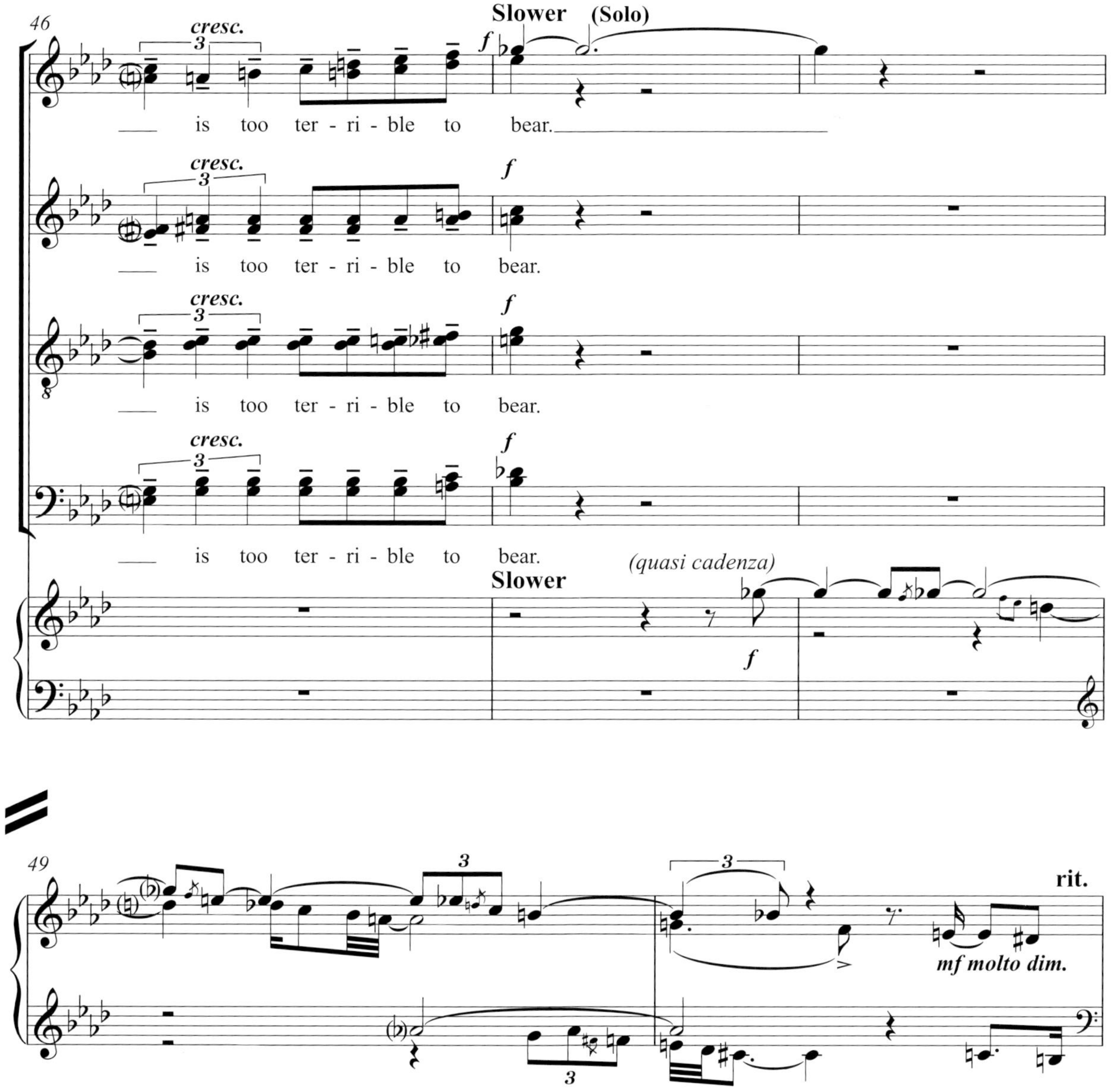

is too ter - ri - ble to bear.

is too ter - ri - ble to bear.

is too ter - ri - ble to bear.

is too ter - ri - ble to bear.

34

green stalks___ lift_____ to play___Through sound - less dew   soft

green stalks   lift_____ to play   Through sound - less dew   soft

lift   to play   Through sound-less dew   sound - less dew

___ to play   Through sound   less dew   sound - less dew

orch - es - tras   of   scent   As   flow - ers

orch - es - tras   of   scent   As   flow - ers

soft   orch - es - tras   of   scent   As

soft   orch - es - tras   of   scent   As

would be the same. Just___ then the
would be the same. Just___ then the
would be the same. Just then the
would be the same. Just then the

gar-de-ner___ spoke one word: my name.
gard-en-er spoke one word: my name.
gard-en-er spoke one word: my name.
gard-en-er spoke one word: my name.

THE COMPOSER WRITES

This carol began life around 2008 as *Carol for Two Boys' Voices*, its scoring inspired by 'O dive custos' of Purcell, with which Francis and I were rather taken at the time. However, not only the refrain form of the traditional 'carol' but also Francis' text, which juxtaposes touching intimacy with a more cosmic aspect, seemed to me to call for the use of lower voices as well (although the treble duet remains integral). Thus the piece was renamed *Questions*; and Francis was most gracious in adapting his conception. I consciously aimed here at an approachable diatonic idiom, so effectively used in many contemporary carols – although a more chromatic language almost inevitably asserts itself as the piece progresses, returning to innocent purity at the end. The rocking accompaniment (initially conceived for piano or organ) speaks for itself; astute observers may notice the influence of the short Bruckner motet I was teaching to my A-level class as I wrote the final section.

In 2019, Sir Stephen Cleobury retired after half a century of greatly distinguished service to church music. A little part of that, happily, involved conducting and recording the collection of anthems by Francis and myself – and so it seemed fitting to write one more piece for him before his retirement. That piece is the *Anthem for Easter Day*. (As it happens, Easter remained unmarked in the collection, unless one counts the *Anthem for Christ the King*.) Francis' text focussed on a more personal, less overtly triumphant, quality to the Resurrection story, seen from the view of Mary Magdalen, and my setting tried to reflect that, from the somewhat sombre F minor opening of the first eight lines evoking shades of black and white to the anthem's gentle conclusion in colour and scents of that new spring dawn.

Having included a significant organ part in most of the anthems, I found myself undecided whether to include one here. As it turns out, the organ functions as a counterpoint to the choir, sometimes dramatic but with their synthesis ultimately achieved. It is my hope that the piece might add in its way to the Easter repertoire.

Conductor-composer and poet share a moment during the interval of the concert in Oxford's Sheldonian Theatre of three of their works: A Legend's Carol *(première),* Four Songs of Time's Return *(première) and* Blitz Requiem *on Saturday 21 October 2017, Francis Warner's 80th Birthday.*

THE POET WRITES

In 1940 we were fighting all-out war with exhausted resources; in the idiom of the time 'with our backs to the wall.' The British army had been defeated, its weapons left on the sands in the retreat from Dunkirk. Nazi Europe, triumphant from North Cape to the Spanish border, waited the signal to invade once the Luftwaffe had cleared our skies of the Royal Air Force. Churchill's great speech of 18th June was clear-eyed:

> 'Upon this battle depends the survival of Christian civilization…The whole fury and might of the enemy must very soon be turned on us…Let us therefore brace ourselves to our duty…'

He was right. Since 10th July for two months we civilians had watched the daily killings in the sky above us which were to continue until the 31st October; but before that date, alongside, from 7th September, Hitler unleashed his night-time Blitzkrieg bombers as well, on industrial targets and civilian centres, and concentrating on London for 57 consecutive sunsets, then intermittently until the spring.

It was at this time, in this extreme context, that Archbishop William Temple published the concluding volume of his masterpiece. Near the end is a calm, apparently simple paragraph on the spiritual basis of the Christian civilization Churchill had so movingly evoked, guiding us to turn our gaze from the overwhelming evil around us and look inwards, at ourselves,[1] perceive this crucifixion of our country through the lens of the crucifixion of Jesus Christ:

> 'The conflict of Light with Darkness is finished. For a moment Darkness seemed to prevail: "this is your hour and the power of darkness" (St. Luke xxii, 53). But the fight was fought out and the victory won: *It is finished* (xix, 30). The date of the triumph of love is Good Friday, not Easter Day. Yet if the story had ended there, the victory would have been barren. What remains is not to win it, but to gather in its fruits. Consequently St. John does not present the Resurrection as a mighty act by which the hosts of evil are routed, but rather as the quiet rising of the sun which has already vanquished night. The atmosphere of the story has all the sweet freshness of dawn on a spring day. Fra Angelico, in his delicious *fresco* of the appearance of the Lord to Mary Magdalene, had perfectly caught its tone and feeling.'[2]

1 Cf. '…one cannot say only that it is a fight of good against evil but also that we have to make ourselves more fit to serve the good cause…' *Some Lambeth Letters 1942–44 by William Temple*, ed. F. S. Temple, Oxford 1963, pp.25–26
2 *Readings in St John's Gospel* by William Temple, vol 2, London, Macmillan, 1940, p.375

Archbishop William Temple apparently answering questions from his Godson Andrew Warner, brother of the poet, 1935

© Billett Potter, 21 October 2017

David Goode rehearsing the Choir and Orchestra for the Sheldonian Theatre concert 2017.

DAVID GOODE was born in 1971 and was educated as a music scholar at Eton College and as organ scholar at King's College, Cambridge, where he took a 1st in Music and subsequently the M.Phil. in Musicology. He was Sub-Organist at Christ Church, Oxford, where he also tutored; while there he wrote his first piece, 'Like as the Hart', for the cathedral choir. Having won several prizes at the 1997 St Albans and 1998 Calgary Organ Competitions, he was a freelance performer and teacher between 2001 and 2003, touring internationally and appearing at venues such as the Royal Festival Hall and the BBC Proms.

Between 2003 and 2005 he was Organist in Residence at First Congregational Church in Los Angeles, where performances of his works included those played by the brass of the LA Philharmonic. His 'Concert Fantasy on themes by Gershwin', written for the new organ of Symphony Hall, Birmingham in 2002, has achieved some popularity. Since 2005 he has been Organist, Head of Keyboard and latterly a house master at Eton College, combining this full-time position with a continuing concert career. He performed at the American Guild of Organists' National Convention in Houston in 2016, and served on the jury of the St Albans Competition in 2017. His recordings of the complete organ works of Bach on the organ of Trinity College, Cambridge are currently being released by Signum.

His partnership with Francis Warner began in 2003 when the choir of King's College performed 'Anthem for St Cecilia's Day'; the collection now numbers seven anthems, a carol and a set of organ variations, all variously performed in Oxford, Cambridge and Eton, and recorded by King's on OXRECS. *Blitz Requiem* was performed by the Bach Choir and RPO under David Hill at St Paul's Cathedral in September 2013, and broadcast on Classic FM; *Eight Sonnets* was premièred in 2015, and *Four Songs of Time's Return* (a song-cycle with orchestra) and the Christmas cantata *A Legend's Carol* in the Sheldonian Theatre in Oxford in 2017.

© Billett Potter, 21 October 2017

FRANCIS WARNER, M.A., D.Litt., Hon. D.Mus., born 1937, is Emeritus Fellow of St Peter's College, Oxford, and Residential Honorary Fellow of St Catharine's College, Cambridge, where in the 1950s he was a Choral Exhibitioner and subsequently taught before moving to St Peter's in 1965. He divides his time between these two colleges.

Educated at Christ's Hospital and the London College of Music, at Cambridge he conducted his own re-scoring of Honegger's *King David* in King's College Chapel for two performances in 1958. In 2003 the recording of this concert was issued as a Landmark Recording CD by OxRecs Digital (OXCD-94).

In 2015 Decca issued in a box set of 29 CDs *The Complete Argo Recordings of the Choir of King's College, Cambridge 1954–1973* introduced by Francis Warner recalling the years when Boris Ord was choirmaster, and John Rutter those when Sir David Willcocks was in charge.

Sixteen of Warner's plays, his *Collected Poems 1960–1984*, *Nightingales: Poems 1985–1996*, and *By the Cam and the Isis 1954–2000* (two long poems) are published by Colin Smythe Ltd, who also publishes *Six Anthems* by David Goode and Francis Warner (with accompanying CD of King's College Choir under Stephen Cleobury singing all six anthems in their liturgical context), and also their *Blitz Requiem* performed by the Bach Choir with the Royal Philharmonic Orchestra in St Paul's Cathedral, London, September 2013 commemorating the 70th anniversary of the Blitz and subsequent five years aerial bombardment of the British Isles.

Colin Smythe Ltd also publishes, with CD, their most recent collaborations, the song cycle *Eight Sonnets*, written for Richard Lloyd Morgan and sung by him at his retirement concert as Chaplain of King's in 2015 with the composer at the piano; and a song cycle on the seasons of the year *Four Songs of Time's Return*, performed in 2017 with *A Legend's Carol* and *Blitz Requiem* in Oxford's Sheldonian Theatre with the Oxford Symphony Orchestra conducted by David Goode.

SIR STEPHEN CLEOBURY, born in 1948, began his musical education as a chorister at Worcester Cathedral. He became organ student at St John's College, Cambridge, and subsequently Organist of St Matthew's, Northampton, Sub-Organist of Westminster Abbey and Master of Music of Westminster Cathedral, before taking up his appointment as Organist and Director of Music at King's College, Cambridge in 1982. Between 1995 and 2007 he was also Chief Conductor of the BBC Singers. He is now their Conductor Laureate.

At King's he has sought to maintain and enhance the reputation of the world-famous Choir, broadening the daily service repertoire, commissioning new music from leading composers, principally for *A Festival of Nine Lessons and Carols*, and developing its activities in broadcasting, recording and touring. He introduced the annual festival, *Easter at King's*, from which the BBC regularly broadcasts, and the series *Concerts at King's*, which brings to the Chapel many world-class performers.

His influence has extended beyond King's through the many organ scholars he has trained: the choirs at Norwich Cathedral, St George's Chapel, Windsor, Trinity College, Cambridge, New College, Oxford, St Mary's Cathedral, Limerick, and St Thomas's Church, New York City are all run by former organ scholars of Stephen, while other choral and organ scholars who have passed through the Choir during Stephen's time now pursue careers as conductors, organ soloists (including David Goode) and opera singers. During his many years as Conductor of the Cambridge University Musical Society in which he conducted most of the major works for chorus and orchestra, he nurtured generations of young musicians. He became the Society's first Conductor Laureate in 2016.

Sir Stephen has played his part in serving a number of organisations in his field. He is a past President of the Royal College of Organists and of the Incorporated Association of Organists; he is President of the Friends of Cathedral Music and of the Herbert Howells Society. Appointed CBE in 2009, he received an honorary doctorate from the University of York in 2018. In 2019 he was awarded a knighthood for services to choral music.

Ten Scores with CDs by David Goode and Francis Warner
Published by Colin Smythe Ltd

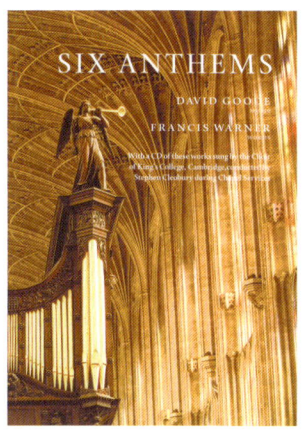

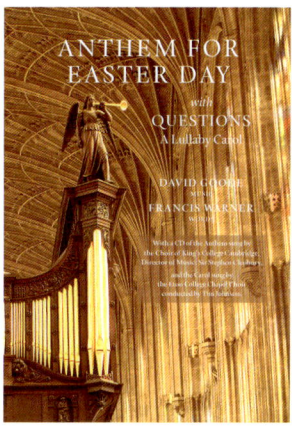

Six Anthems
choir with organ

Blitz Requiem
orchestral score, also in
conductor's score and
vocal score

Anthem for Easter Day
choir with organ

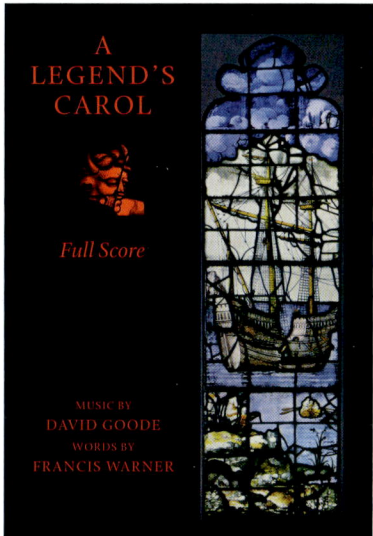

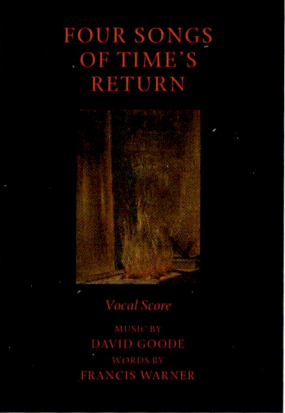

Eight Sonnets
baritone with piano

A Legend's Carol
orchestral score,
also in vocal score

*Four Songs of
Time's Return*
soprano and baritone
vocal score, also in
orchestral score